Ancient Egyptian Mysteries and Hieroglyphics, Modern Freemasonry & Initiation of the Pyramid

By Henry Ridgely Evans, Manly P. Hall,
Albert G. Mackey and George Smith

Copyright © 2019 Lamp of Trismegistus. All rights reserved. No part of this publication may be reproduced or transmitted in any form or by any means, electronic or mechanical, including photocopying, recording, or by any information storage and retrieval system, without permission in writing from Lamp of Trismegistus. Reviewers may quote brief passages.

ISBN: 978-1-63118-430-7

Esoteric Classics

Other Books in this Series and Related Titles

Magical Essays and Instructions by Florence Farr
(978-1-63118-418-5)

Ancient Mysteries and Secret Societies by Manly P. Hall
(978-1-63118-410-9)

The First and Second Gospels of the Infancy of Jesus Christ
by Thomas and James (978-1-63118-415-4)

Lost Atlantis and the Gods of Antiquity & Plato's History of Atlantis
by Carolus Kiesewetterus and Manly P. Hall
(978-1-63118-431-4)

The Human Aura: Astral Colors and Thought Forms by Swami
Panchadasi and William Walker Atkinson (978-1-63118-419-2)

The Book of the Watchers by Enoch (978-1-63118-416-1)

The Smoky God or A Voyage to the Inner World
by Willis George Emerson (978-1-63118-423-9)

Rosa Alchemica, The Tables of Law & The Adoration of the Magi
by William Butler Yeats (978-1-63118-421-5)

The Lives of Adam and Eve by Moses (978-1-63118-414-7)

Occult Symbolism of Animals, Insects, Reptiles, Fish and Birds
by Manly P. Hall (978-1-63118-420-8)

The Feminine Occult by various authors (978-1-63118-711-7)

Thirty-One Hymns to the Star Goddess by Frater Achad
(978-1-63118-422-2)

Audio Versions are also Available on Audible and iTunes

Table of Contents

Introduction…7

Egyptian Mysteries and Modern Freemasonry
by Henry Ridgely Evans
Part I…9
Part II…15

-oOo-

Initiation of the Pyramid
by Manly P. Hall
Part I: Beginnings…19
Part II: Pyramid Problems…25
Part III: The Sphinx…31
Part IV: The Pyramid Mysteries…37

-oOo-

Masonic Hieroglyphics
by George Smith…45

-oOo-

The Ancient Mysteries
by Albert G. Mackey…53

Introduction

The word "esoteric" can be difficult to define. Esotericism in general can be seen less as a system of beliefs and more as a category, which encompasses numerous, different systems of beliefs. It's a bit of juxtaposition, since the word "esoteric" indicates something that few people know about, while the term itself broadly covers numerous philosophies, practices, areas of study and belief systems.

In a greater sense, Esotericism acts as a storehouse for secret knowledge, which is often considered ancient (by *tradition, if not by fact),* passed down from generation to generation, in private. At various times in history, simply possessing the knowledge of some of these subjects, was considered illegal and a jailable offence, if discovered. This usually included such general topics as Alchemy, Qabalah, Hermeticism, Occultism, Ceremonial Magic, Astrology, Divination, Rosicrucianism and so on. Collectively, these areas of study were often referred to as the esoteric sciences.

Sometimes, the outer garment of a subject isn't esoteric, while what is hidden beneath it, is. As an example, Freemasonry isn't necessarily esoteric by nature (at *least not anymore),* but certain signs, passwords and handshakes given to the candidate during their initiation, are in fact, esoteric, in the sense that they are hidden from the general public.

Today, in the twenty-first century, such topics are readily available at bookstores across the country, and numerous mainsteam publishers offer beginners guides and coffee-table volumes on many of these subjects, intended for mass appeal. Books like *"The Secret"* have turned previously arcane topics into household knowledge. All that being the case, however, it isn't to say that there still aren't buried secrets to uncover, ancient wisdom being ignored and forgotten mysteries to be explored. In fact, it is often that we are only able to further our own studies by standing on the shoulders of these disappearing giants.

Lamp of Trismegistus is doing its part to help preserve humanity's esoteric history by making some of these classics available to those students who are seeking to unearth the knowledge of these ancient colossi.

So, be sure to check other titles from our *Esoteric Classics* series, as well as our *Occult Fiction*, *Theosophical Classics*, *Foundations of Freemasonry* and our *Christian Apocrypha Series*. You can also download the audio versions of most of these titles from iTunes or Audible.

Egyptian Mysteries and Modern Freemasonry

By Henry Ridgely Evans

Part I

An interesting question now presents itself: What relationship, if any, do the Egyptian Mysteries bear to Freemasonry? Dr. Mackey, a well-known writer on Masonic themes, in an examination of the analogies between the Ancient Mysteries and the rites of modern Freemasonry, lays particular stress upon "the identity of design and method in the two systems, as illustrated by the division—into steps, classes, or degrees—to which both were subjected, viz., *lustration* (purification, or preparation), *initiation,* and *perfection.*"

The "Old Charges" are nearly all unanimous in claiming Egypt as the birthplace of the art of masonry (or mystery). How far the legends of the Craft are to be relied upon in this regard is a matter for learned investigation.

Heckethorne is not very partial to the Fraternity, but he says: "The Mysteries as they have come down to us *and are still perpetuated in a corrupted and aimless manner in Freemasonry,* have chiefly an astronomical bearing."

A hundred or more works have been written to prove that Freemasonry is the *lineal* descendant of the Mysteries. Similar claims have been made in favor of the following systems or sects: (1) The Pythagoreans; (2) The Essenes; (3) The Roman

Collegia; (4) The Culdees; (5) The Druids; (6) The Knights Templar; (7) The Rosicrucians; (8) The Mediaeval Cathedral Builders. The truth of the matter seems to be in favor of the latter,—the Mediaeval operative masons, who built those superb Gothic edifices, such as the cathedrals of Cologne, Rheims, Strassburg, Notre Dame, and Westminster Abbey. Originally an operative institution, Freemasonry became a "speculative society to promote the practice of the moral, fraternal, and charitable principles which had characterized the old organization."

Many noted scholars who were well versed in ancient religions and occult philosophies were initiated into Freemasonry in the seventeenth and eighteenth centuries. Perhaps these students introduced the theosophic symbols of the Neo- Platonists, Cabbalists, Gnostics, and Mediaeval Rosicrucians into the Craft. There is authority for the support of such a belief. Says Gould, in his *History of Freemasonry*: "According to Mackey, an instance of the *transmutation* of Gnostic talismans into Masonic symbols, by a gradual transmission through alchemy, Rosicrucianism, and mediaeval architecture, is afforded by one of the plates of Basil Valentine, the Hermetic philosopher, who flourished in the seventeenth century. This plate, which is hermetic in its design, but is full of Masonic symbolism, represents a winged globe inscribed with a triangle within a square, and on it, reposes a dragon. On the latter stands a human figure of two hands and two heads surrounded by the sun, the moon, and five stars, representing the seven planets. One of the heads is that of a male, the other of a female. The hand attached to the male part of the figure holds the compasses, that to the female a square. The square and compasses thus distributed appear to have convinced Dr. Mackey that originally a phallic meaning was attached to these symbols, as there was to the point within the circle, which in this plate also appears in the center of the globe. "The compasses held by the male figure would represent the male generative principle, and the square held by the female the female productive principle. The subsequent interpretation given to the combined square and compasses was the transmutation from the hermetic talisman to the Masonic symbol."

Just how much was borrowed from older systems by modern scholars, or how much was inherited from the guilds of operative masons, is a mooted question. The "Old Charges" are silent on the subject of the secret work of the Order. In those days the esoteric part of the ritual was better kept. Many writers, however, have claimed that the operative masons of mediaeval times possessed no particular legends or symbols. The ceremony of initiation into a lodge was very simple, the candidate being taught nothing but a few trite ethical lessons, and the grips and words whereby to make himself known to his fellow- craftsmen, when travelling from city to city in quest of work.

From either standpoint—that of inheritance or late borrowing —much of the wisdom of the ancient temples of Egypt and Greece has undoubtedly filtered into the Fraternity, although it has been sadly misunderstood and misinterpreted by Masons in general. The esoteric student, however, is able to draw aside the veil of Isis and discover the true meaning of the symbols and legends of the Craft. Albert Pike, whom no greater unfolder of masonic mysteries ever lived, has done this to a great extent in his remarkable book *The Morals and Dogma of the Scottish Rite*. Robert Hewitt Brown has performed a similar work in his interesting treatise *Stellar Theology and Masonic Astronomy*. Brown emphasizes the astronomical origin of the rites of Freemasonry, tracing them back to the Mysteries. Heckethorne supports this view. It is a very plausible one in some respects, particularly as regards the third degree of Masonry. In almost all of the Mysteries of the ancient world we see this solar allegory cropping out,—the death and resurrection of the sun-god, and the lessons to be drawn therefrom as regards the life of man.

In Freemasonry we have the curious legend of Hiram Abiff, the widow's son. The Hiram who cast the great pillars of brass, Jachim and Boaz, which ornamented the portal of Solomon's Temple, and the numerous holy vessels used in the Jewish ceremonial, was not assassinated. Neither in the Bible nor in the writings of Josephus is there any account of his dying by violence. The story of Grand-Master Hiram Abiff is now regarded as a fable, pure and simple, by all Masonic scholars. It has no historical significance whatever, any more than the story of Isis and Osiris. It is, in the opinion of many eminent authorities, a solar allegory.

When, or how, the legend of Hiram came into the Masonic Fraternity is shrouded in mystery. Some claim that it was inherited from the Egyptian Mysteries, through Jewish, Grecian, or Mithraic channels, being a sort of paraphrase of the Osiris myth. Other writers assert that it was introduced into the

Craft at a late date, probably during the speculative epoch. The astronomical significance of the legend has been lost to Freemasonry, so far as the explanations of the ritual are concerned. It is a pity! Masonry should not only be in possession of ethical and spiritual truths, but scientific as well. Nothing is grander than the contemplation of the heavenly bodies, and facts connected with their mysterious orbits.

Albert Pike shows that the name "Hiram" is a corruption of *Khairum* or *Khurum,* a compound word, having reference, in one of its meanings, to the sun. *Khairum* in Hebrew translates "was raised up to life, or living." In Arabic *Arm,* an unused root, meant, "was high," or "made great," or "exalted." And, also in Arabic, *Hirm* means an ox, the symbol of the sun in Taurus, at the vernal equinox. I have not the space to follow the learned author in all of his philological dissertations upon this point. The reader is referred to the work itself, *Morals and Dogma,* for detailed explanations. The raising of Hiram (*or the sun*) from the grave of winter to life and power is the substance of the allegory.

On the 21st of June, when the sun arrives at the summer solstice, the constellation *Leo*—being but 30° in advance of the sun— appears to be leading the way, and to aid by his powerful paw in lifting the sun up to the summit of the zodiacal arch. April and May are therefore said to fail in their attempt to raise the sun; June alone succeeds, by the aid of *Leo*. When, at a more remote period, the summer solstice was *in Leo,* and the sun actually entered the stars of that constellation at the time of his exaltation, the connection was more intimate, and the allegory still more perfect.

Says Brown: "The *visible* connection between the constellation *Leo* and the return of the sun to his place of power and glory, at the summit of the Royal Arch of heaven, was the principal reason why that constellation was held in such high esteem and reverence by the ancients. The astrologers distinguished *Leo* as the 'sole house of the sun,' and taught that the world was created when the sun was in that sign. 'The lion was adored in the East and West by the Egyptians and the Mexicans. The Chief Druid of Britain was styled a lion. The national banner of the ancient Persians bore the device of the sun in Leo. A lion couchant with the sun rising at his back was sculptured on their palaces.'

"After the sun leaves Leo, the days begin to grow unequivocally shorter as the sun declines toward the autumnal equinox, to be again slain by the *three* autumnal months, lie dead through the *three* winter ones, and be raised again by the three vernal ones. Each year the great tragedy is repeated, and the glorious resurrection takes place.

"Thus, as long as this allegory is remembered, the leading truths of astronomy will be perpetuated, and the sublime doctrine of the immortal nature of man, and other great moral lessons they are thus made to teach, will be illustrated and preserved."

Part II

There is an emblematic figure, copied by Pluche from the collection of Mountfancon, and painted on a mummy case at the Austin friars' of La Place des Victoires, which represents the death and resurrection of Osiris, and the beginning, progress, and end of the inundation of the Nile. Speaking of the figure, John Fellows says, *"The sign of the lion is transformed into a couch, upon which Osiris is laid out as dead; under which are four canopi of various capacities, indicating the state of the Nile at different periods. The first is terminated by the head of the dog-star, which gives warning of the approach of the overflow of the river; the second, by the head of a hawk, the symbol of the Etesian wind, which tends to swell the waters; the third, by the head of a heron, the sign of the south wind, which contributes to propel the water into the Mediterranean sea; and the fourth, by that of the virgin; which indicates that when the sun had passed that sign, the inundation would have nearly subsided*

"To the above is superadded a large Anubis, who with an emphatic gesture turning towards Isis who has an empty throne on her head, intimates that the sun, by the aid of the lion, had cleared the difficult pass of the Tropic of Cancer, and was now in the sign of the latter, and, although in a state of exhaustion, would soon be in a condition to proceed on his way to the South; at the same time gives to the husbandman the important warning of retiring to avoid the inundation. The empty throne is indicative of its being vacated by the supposed death of Osiris.

"The raising of Hiram is evidently copied from this fable....

"It may be remarked that the lamentations uttered for the death of grand master Hiram is in exact accordance with the customs of the

Egyptians in their celebrations of the fabled death of Osiris, the sun; of the Phoenicians for the loss of Adonis; and of the Greeks, in their mystic rites of the Eleusinian Ceres.

"*It is through the instrumentality of Leo that Osiris, the sun, is retrieved from his perilous condition. The strong paw of the lion wrests him from the clutches of Typhon, and places him in his wonted course. Anubis, the dog-star, is the herald of this event.*"

An ancient Egyptian drawing, found in the sarcophagus of one of the kings of Egypt, entombed in the pyramid erected to his memory, constitutes "*startling testimony of the entire correctness of the astronomical solution of the legend of Osiris and that of Hiram.*"

Stellar Theology thus explains the emblem: "The form that lies dead before the altar is that of Osiris, the personified sun-god, whom the candidate represents in the drama of initiation, lying dead at the winter solstice. The cross upon his breast refers to the great celestial cross, or intersection of the celestial equator by the ecliptic. The figure of the lion grasping the dead sun-god by the hand alludes to the constellation Leo and the summer solstice, at which point the sun is raised to life and glory, as has been just explained in the allegory of the resurrection of the sun, and denotes that the candidate is about to be raised from a symbolical death to life and power by the grip of the lion's paw. This is made clearly manifest from the fact that the lion holds in his other paw the ancient Egyptian symbol of eternal life, or the *Crux Ansata*. The tablet at the feet of the candidate has inscribed upon it in hieroglyphics the sacred names of *Anton* and of *Mut,* the wife of *Amon Ra,* and probably that of the royal candidate. The figure erect at the altar is that of the Grand Hierophant, attired as Isis, with the vacant throne upon his head, emblematic of the departed sun-god. She has her hand raised in an attitude of command, her arm forming a right angle; her eyes fixed upon the emblematic lion as she gives the sign of command that the candidate be raised from death and darkness to light and life. The objects on the altar are two of those peculiar-shaped jars, with pointed bases, in which wine was kept, and which, the same author says, 'always had their place on the altar of the gods'. The emblem placed between the votive jars of wine is more obscure. It may be the *thyrsus,* but is more probably a floral offering. There can be no doubt but that the whole device is a symbolical picture of the initiation of some important person into the Mysteries, not of Osiris, however, as Paterson thinks, but of Isis, who, represented by the Grand Hierophant, stands behind the altar, giving the command to raise from death Osiris, who lies before it."

The reader will find in *Stellar Theology* the astronomical significance of many other important Masonic symbols—symbols that teach not only scientific facts, but typify the unity of God, and the immortal progress of the soul. He says: "Though in all parts of our ritual, from the threshold to the altar to the *penetralia* (*as in the ancient Mysteries, from which Freemasonry has descended*), the profoundest truths of science and true religion are taught and illustrated by astronomical allegories, yet nowhere do we find, even in its most ancient portions, any prayers, invocations, or adorations, addressed to the heavenly bodies themselves. The sun and the hosts of heaven are only used as emblems of the Deity... The Mysteries themselves, in their primitive and uncorrupted form, taught the unity of God and the immortality of man as their cardinal doctrines, and that the sun was but a symbol of Him whom 'the sun, moon, and stars obey, and beneath whose all-seeing eye even comets perform their stupendous revolutions'."

"In the great mysteries of Eleusis," says Albert G. Mackey, "we learn from St. Chrysostom, as well as other authorities, that the temple of initiation was symbolic of the universe, and we know that one of the officers (the *dadouchos,* or torch-bearer) represented the sun." The myth of Demeter searching for her daughter in the realms of Pluto, or the underworld, is the old solar allegory with a Grecian tinge.

All places of initiation in the ancient days typified the universe—Hindu, Egyptian, Persian, and Grecian. The masonic lodge is a symbol of the world and the three principal officers represent the sun at its rising, its setting, and its meridian height.

The Initiation of the Pyramid

By Manly P. Hall

PART I

BEGINNINGS

Supreme among the wonders of antiquity, unrivaled by the achievements of later architects and builders, the Great Pyramid of Gizeh bears mute witness to an unknown civilization which, having completed its predestined span, passed into oblivion. Eloquent in its silence, inspiring in its majesty, divine in its simplicity, the Great Pyramid is indeed a sermon in stone. Its magnitude overwhelms the puny sensibilities of man. Among the shifting sands of time it stands as a fitting emblem of eternity itself. Who were the illumined mathematicians who planned its parts and dimensions, the master craftsmen who supervised its construction, the skilled artisans who trued its blocks of stone?

The earliest and best-known account of the building of the Great Pyramid is that given by that highly revered but somewhat imaginative historian, Herodotus. "The pyramid was built in steps, battlement-wise, as it is called, or, according to others, altar-wise. After laying the stones for the base, they raised the remaining stones to their places by means of machines formed of short wooden planks. The first machine raised them from the ground to the top of the first step. On this there was another machine, which received the stone upon its arrival, and conveyed it to the second step, whence a third machine advanced it still higher. Either they had as many machines as there were steps in the pyramid, or possibly they had but a single machine, which, being easily moved, was transferred from tier to tier as the stone rose. Both accounts are given, and therefore I mention both. The upper portion of the pyramid was finished first, then the middle, and finally the part which was lowest and nearest the ground. There is an inscription in Egyptian characters on the pyramid which records the quantity of radishes, onions, and garlick consumed by the labourers who constructed it; and I perfectly well remember that the interpreter who read the writing to me said that the money expended in this way was 1600 talents of silver. If this then is a true record, what a vast sum must have been spent on the iron tools used in the work, and on the feeding and clothing of the labourers, considering the length of time the work lasted, which has already been stated [ten years], and the additional time--no small space, I imagine--which must have been occupied by the quarrying of the stones, their conveyance, and the formation of the underground apartments."

While his account is extremely colorful, it is apparent that the Father of History, for reasons which he doubtless considered sufficient, concocted a fraudulent story to conceal the true origin and purpose of the Great Pyramid. This is but one of several instances in his writings which would lead the thoughtful reader to suspect that Herodotus himself was an initiate of the Sacred Schools and consequently obligated to preserve inviolate the secrets of the ancient orders. The theory advanced by Herodotus and now generally accepted that the Pyramid was the tomb of the Pharaoh Cheops cannot be substantiated. In fact, Manetho, Eratosthenes, and Diodorus Siculus all differ from Herodotus--as well as from each other--regarding the name of the builder of this supreme edifice. The sepulchral vault, which, according to the Lepsius Law of pyramid construction, should have been finished at the same time as the monument or sooner, was never completed. There is no proof that the building was erected by the Egyptians, for the elaborate carvings with which the burial chambers of Egyptian royalty are almost invariably ornamented are entirely lacking and it embodies none of the elements of their architecture or decoration, such as inscriptions, images, cartouches, paintings, and other distinctive features associated with dynastic mortuary art. The only hieroglyphics to be found within the Pyramid are a few builders' marks sealed up in the *chambers of construction*, first opened by Howard Vyse. These apparently were painted upon the stones before they were set in position, for in a number of instances the marks were either inverted or disfigured by the operation of fitting the blocks together. While Egyptologists have attempted to identify the crude dabs of paint as cartouches of Cheops, it is almost inconceivable that this ambitious ruler would have permitted his royal name to suffer such indignities. As the most eminent authorities on the subject are still uncertain as to the true meaning of these crude markings, whatever proof they might be that the building was erected during the fourth dynasty is certainly offset by the sea shells at the base of the Pyramid which Mr. Gab advances as evidence that it was erected before the Deluge--a theory substantiated by the much-abused

Arabian traditions. One Arabian historian declared that the Pyramid was built by the Egyptian sages as a refuge against the Flood, while another proclaimed it to have been the treasure house of the powerful antediluvian king Sheddad Ben Ad. A panel of hieroglyphs over the entrance, which the casual observer might consider to afford a solution of the mystery, unfortunately dates back no further than A.D. 1843, having been cut at that time by Dr. Lepsius as a tribute to the King of Prussia.

Caliph al Mamoun, an illustrious descendant of the Prophet, inspired by stories of the immense treasures sealed within its depths, journeyed from Bagdad to Cairo, A.D. 820, with a great force of workmen to open the mighty Pyramid. When Caliph al Mamoun first reached the foot of the "Rock of Ages" and gazed up at its smooth glistening surface, a tumult of emotions undoubtedly racked his soul. The casing stones must have been in place at the time of his visit, for the Caliph could find no indication of an entrance--four perfectly smooth surfaces confronted him. Following vague rumors, he set his followers to work on the north side of the Pyramid, with instructions to keep on cutting and chiseling until they discovered something. To the Moslems with their crude instruments and vinegar it was a herculean effort to tunnel a full hundred feet through the limestone. Many times they were on the point of rebellion, but the word of the Caliph was law and the hope of a vast fortune buoyed them up.

At last on the eve of total discouragement fate came to their rescue. A great stone was heard to fall somewhere in the wall near the toiling and disgruntled Arabs. Pushing on toward the sound with renewed enthusiasm, they finally broke into the descending passage which leads into the subterranean chamber. They then chiseled their way around the great stone portcullis which had fallen into a position barring their progress, and attacked and removed one after another the granite plugs which for a while continued to slide down the passage leading from the Queen's Chamber above.

Finally no more blocks descended and the way was clear for the followers of the Prophet. But where were the treasures? From room to room the frantic workmen rushed, looking in vain for loot. The discontent of the Moslems reached such a height that Caliph al Mamoun--who had inherited much of the wisdom of his illustrious father, the Caliph al Raschid--sent to Bagdad for funds, which he caused to be secretly buried near the entrance of the Pyramid. He then ordered his men to dig at that spot and great was their rejoicing when the treasure was discovered, the workmen being deeply impressed by the wisdom of the antediluvian monarch who had carefully estimated their wages and thoughtfully caused the exact amount to be buried for their benefit!

The Caliph then returned to the city of his fathers and the Great Pyramid was left to the mercy of succeeding generations. In the ninth century the sun's rays striking the highly polished surfaces of the original casing stones caused each side of the Pyramid to appear as a dazzling triangle of light. Since that time, all but two of these casing stones have disappeared. Investigation has resulted in their discovery, recut and resurfaced, in the walls of Mohammedan mosques and palaces in various parts of Cairo and its environs.

PART II

PYRAMID PROBLEMS

C. Piazzi Smyth asks: "Was the Great Pyramid, then, erected before the invention of hieroglyphics, and previous to the birth of the Egyptian religion?" Time may yet prove that the upper chambers of the Pyramid were a sealed mystery before the establishment of the Egyptian empire. In the subterranean chamber, however, are markings which indicate that the Romans gained admission there. In the light of the secret philosophy of the Egyptian initiates, W. W. Harmon, by a series of extremely complicated yet exact mathematical calculations; determines that the first ceremonial of the Pyramid was performed 68,890 years ago on the occasion when the star Vega for the first time sent its ray down the descending passage into the pit. The actual building of the Pyramid was accomplished in the period of from ten to fifteen years immediately preceding this date.

While such figures doubtless will evoke the ridicule of modern Egyptologists, they are based upon an exhaustive study of the principles of sidereal mechanics as incorporated into the structure of the Pyramid by its initiated builders. If the casing stones were in position at the beginning of the ninth century, the so-called erosion marks upon the outside were not due to water. The theory also that the salt upon the interior stones of the Pyramid is evidence that the building was once submerged is weakened by the scientific fact that this kind of stone is subject to exudations of salt. While the building may have been submerged, at least in part, during the many thousands of years since its erection, the evidence adduced to prove this point is not conclusive.

The Great Pyramid was built of limestone and granite throughout, the two kinds of rock being combined in a peculiar and significant manner. The stones were trued with the utmost precision, and the cement used was of such remarkable quality that it is now practically as hard as the stone itself. The limestone blocks were sawed with bronze saws, the teeth of which were diamonds or other jewels. The chips from the stones were piled against the north side of the plateau on which the structure stands, where they form an additional buttress to aid in supporting the weight of the structure. The entire Pyramid is an example of perfect orientation and actually squares the circle. This last is accomplished by dropping a vertical line from the apex of the Pyramid to its base line. If this vertical line be considered as the radius of an imaginary circle, the length of the circumference of such a circle will be found to equal the sum of the base lines of the four sides of the Pyramid.

If the passage leading to the King's Chamber and the Queen's Chamber was sealed up thousands of years before the Christian Era, those later admitted into the Pyramid Mysteries must have received their initiations in subterranean galleries now unknown. Without such galleries there could have been no possible means of ingress or egress, since the single surface entrance was completely dosed with casing stones. If not blocked by the mass of the Sphinx or concealed in some part of that image, the secret entrance may be either in one of the adjacent temples or upon the sides of the limestone plateau.

Attention is called to the granite plugs filling the ascending passageway to the Queen's Chamber which Caliph al Mamoun was forced practically to pulverize before he could clear a way into the upper chambers. C. Piazzi Smyth notes that the positions of the stones demonstrate that they were set in place from above--which made it necessary for a considerable number of workmen to depart from the upper chambers. How did they do it? Smyth believes they descended through the well (see diagram), dropping the ramp stone into place behind them. He further contends that robbers probably used the well as a means of getting into the upper chambers. The ramp stone having been set in a bed of plaster, the robbers were forced to break through it, leaving a jagged opening. Mr. Dupré, an architect who has spent years investigating the pyramids, differs from Smyth, however, in that he believes the well itself to be a robbers' hole, being the first successful attempt made to enter the upper chambers from the subterranean chamber, then the only open section of the Pyramid.

Mr. Dupré bases his conclusion upon the fact that the well is merely a rough hole and the grotto an irregular chamber, without any evidence of the architectural precision with which the remainder of the structure was erected. The diameter of the well also precludes the possibility of its having been dug downward; it must have been gouged out from below, and the grotto was necessary to supply air to the thieves. It is inconceivable that the Pyramid builders would break one of their own ramp stones and leave its broken surface and a gaping hole in the side wall of their otherwise perfect gallery. If the well is a robbers' hole, it may explain why the Pyramid was empty when Caliph al Mamoun entered it and what happened to the missing coffer lid. A careful examination of the so-called unfinished subterranean chamber, which must have been the base of operations for the robbers, might disclose traces of their presence or show where they piled the rubble which must have accumulated as a result of their operations. While it is not entirely clear by what entrance the robbers reached the subterranean chamber, it is improbable that they used the descending passageway.

There is a remarkable niche in the north wall of the Queen's Chamber which the Mohammedan guides glibly pronounce to be a shrine. The general shape of this niche, however, with its walls converging by a series of overlaps like those of the Grand Gallery, would indicate that originally it had been intended as a passageway. Efforts made to explore this niche have been nonproductive, but Mr. Dupré believes an entrance to exist here through which--if the well did not exist at the time--the workmen made their exit from the Pyramid after dropping the stone plugs into the ascending gallery.

Biblical scholars have contributed a number of most extraordinary conceptions regarding the Great Pyramid. This ancient edifice has been identified by them as Joseph's granary (despite its hopelessly inadequate capacity); as the tomb prepared for the unfortunate Pharaoh of the Exodus who could not be buried there because his body was never recovered from the Red Sea; and finally as a perpetual confirmation of the infallibility of the numerous prophecies contained in the Authorized Version!

PART III

THE SPHINX

Although the Great Pyramid, as Ignatius Donnelly has demonstrated, is patterned after an antediluvian type of architecture, examples of which are to be found in nearly every part of the world, the Sphinx (*Hu*) is typically Egyptian. The stele between its paws states the Sphinx is an image of the Sun God, Harmackis, which was evidently made in the similitude of the Pharaoh during whose reign it was chiseled. The statue was restored and completely excavated by Tahutmes IV as the result of a vision in which the god had appeared and declared himself oppressed by the weight of the sand about his body. The broken beard of the Sphinx was discovered during excavations between the front paws. The steps leading up to the sphinx and also the temple and altar between the paws are much later additions, probably Roman, for it is known that the Romans reconstructed many Egyptian antiquities. The shallow depression in the crown of the head, once thought to be the terminus of a closed up passageway leading from the Sphinx to the Great Pyramid, was merely intended to help support a headdress now missing.

Metal rods have been driven into the Sphinx in a vain effort to discover chambers or passages within its body. The major part of the Sphinx is a single stone, but the front paws have been built up of smaller stones. The Sphinx is about 200 feet long, 70 feet high, and 38 feet wide across the shoulders. The main stone from which it was carved is believed by some to have been transported from distant quarries by methods unknown, while others assert it to be native rock, possibly an outcropping somewhat resembling the form into which it was later carved. The theory once advanced that both the Pyramid and the Sphinx were built from artificial stones made on the spot has been abandoned. A careful analysis of the limestone shows it to be composed of small sea creatures called *mummulites*.

The popular supposition that the Sphinx was the true portal of the Great Pyramid, while it survives with surprising tenacity, has never been substantiated. P. Christian presents this theory as follows, basing it in part upon the authority of Iamblichus:

"The Sphinx of Gizeh, says the author of the Traité des Mystères, served as the entrance to the sacred subterranean chambers in which the trials of the initiate were undergone. This entrance, obstructed in our day by sands and rubbish, may still be traced between the forelegs of the crouched colossus. It was formerly closed by a bronze gate whose secret spring could be operated only by the Magi. It was guarded by public respect: and a sort of religious fear maintained its inviolability better than armed protection would have done. In the belly of the Sphinx were cut out galleries leading to the subterranean part of the Great Pyramid. These galleries were so artfully crisscrossed along their course to the Pyramid that in setting forth into the passage without a guide through this network, one ceaselessly and inevitably returned to the starting point." (See *Histoire de la Magie*.)

Unfortunately, the bronze door referred to cannot be found, nor is there any evidence that it ever existed. The passing centuries have wrought many changes in the colossus, however, and the original opening may have been closed.

Nearly all students of the subject believe that subterranean chambers exist beneath the Great Pyramid. Robert Ballard writes: "The priests of the Pyramids of Lake Mœris had their vast subterranean residences. It appears to me more than probable that those of Gizeh were similarly provided. And I may go further:--Out of these very caverns may have been excavated the limestone of which the Pyramids were built. * * * In the bowels of the limestone ridge on which the Pyramids are built will yet be found, I feel convinced, ample information as to their uses. A good diamond drill with two or three hundred feet of rods is what is wanted to test this, and the solidarity of the Pyramids at the same time." (See *The Solution of the Pyramid Problem*.)

Mr. Ballard's theory of extensive underground apartments and quarries brings up an important problem in architectonics. The Pyramid builders were too farsighted to endanger the permanence of the Great Pyramid by placing over five million tons of limestone and granite on any but a solid foundation. It is therefore reasonably certain that such chambers or passageways as may exist beneath the building are relatively insignificant, like those within the body of the structure, which occupy less than one sixteen-hundredth of the cubic contents of the Pyramid.

The Sphinx was undoubtedly erected for symbolical purposes at the instigation of the priestcraft. The theories that the uræus upon its forehead was originally the finger of an immense sundial and that both the Pyramid and the Sphinx were used to measure time, the seasons, and the precession of the equinoxes are ingenious but not wholly convincing. If this great creature was erected to obliterate the ancient passageway leading into the subterranean temple of the Pyramid, its symbolism would be most appropriate. In comparison with the overwhelming size and dignity of the Great Pyramid, the Sphinx is almost insignificant. Its battered face, upon which may still be seen vestiges of the red paint with which the figure was originally covered, is disfigured beyond recognition. Its nose was broken off by a fanatical Mohammedan, lest the followers of the Prophet be led into idolatry. The very nature of its construction and the present repairs necessary to prevent the head from falling off indicate that it could not have survived the great periods of time which have elapsed since the erection of the Pyramid.

To the Egyptians, the Sphinx was the symbol of strength and intelligence. It was portrayed as androgynous to signify that they recognized the initiates and gods as partaking of both the positive and negative creative powers. Gerald Massey writes: "This is the secret of the Sphinx. The orthodox sphinx of Egypt is masculine in front and feminine behind. So is the image of Sut-Typhon, a type of horn and tail, male in front and female behind. The Pharaohs, who wore the tail of the Lioness or Cow behind them, were male in front and female behind. Like the Gods they included the dual totality of Being in one person, born of the Mother, but of both sexes as the Child." (See *The Natural Genesis.*)

Most investigators have ridiculed the Sphinx and, without even deigning to investigate the great colossus, have turned their attention to the more overwhelming mystery of the Pyramid.

PART IV

THE PYRAMID MYSTERIES

The word pyramid is popularly supposed to be derived from πῦρ, fire, thus signifying that it is the symbolic representation of the One Divine Flame, the life of every creature. John Taylor believes the word pyramid to mean a "measure of wheat, " while C. Piazzi Smyth favors the Coptic meaning, "a division into ten." The initiates of old accepted the pyramid form as the ideal symbol of both the secret doctrine and those institutions established for its dissemination. Both pyramids and mounds are antitypes of the Holy Mountain, or High Place of God, which was believed to stand in the "midst" of the earth. John P. Lundy relates the Great Pyramid to the fabled Olympus, further assuming that its subterranean passages correspond to the tortuous byways of Hades.

The square base of the Pyramid is a constant reminder that the House of Wisdom is firmly founded upon Nature and her immutable laws. "The Gnostics," writes Albert Pike, "claimed that the whole edifice of their science rested on a square whose angles were: Σιγη, Silence; Βυθος, Profundity; Νους, Intelligence; and Αληθεια Truth." (See *Morals and Dogma*.) The sides of the Great Pyramid face the four cardinal angles, the latter signifying according to Eliphas Levi the extremities of heat and cold (south and north) and the extremities of light and darkness (east and west). The base of the Pyramid further represents the four material elements or substances from the combinations of which the quaternary body of man is formed.

From each side of the square there rises a triangle, typifying the threefold divine being enthroned within every quaternary material nature. If each base line be considered a square from which ascends a threefold spiritual power, then the sum of the lines of the four faces (12) and the four hypothetical squares (16) constituting the base is 28, the sacred number of the lower world. If this be added to the three septenaries composing the sun (21), it equals 49, the square of 7 and the number of the universe.

The twelve signs of the zodiac, like the Governors' of the lower worlds, are symbolized by the twelve lines of the four triangles--the faces of the Pyramid. In the midst of each face is one of the beasts of Ezekiel, and the structure as a whole becomes the Cherubim. The three main chambers of the Pyramid are related to the heart, the brain, and the generative system--the spiritual centers of the human constitution. The triangular form of the Pyramid also is similar to the posture assumed by the body during the ancient meditative exercises. The Mysteries taught that the divine energies from the gods descended upon the top of the Pyramid, which was likened to an inverted tree with its branches below and its roots at the apex. From this inverted tree the divine wisdom is disseminated by streaming down the diverging sides and radiating throughout the world.

The size of the capstone of the Great Pyramid cannot be accurately determined, for, while most investigators have assumed that it was once in place, no vestige of it now remains. There is a curious tendency among the builders of great religious edifices to leave their creations unfinished, thereby signifying that God alone is complete. The capstone--if it existed--was itself a miniature pyramid, the apex of which again would be capped by a smaller block of similar shape, and so on *ad infinitum*. The capstone therefore is the epitome of the entire structure. Thus, the Pyramid may be likened to the universe and the capstone to man. Following the chain of analogy, the mind is the capstone of man, the spirit the capstone of the mind, and God--the epitome of the whole--the capstone of the spirit. As a rough and unfinished block, man is taken from the quarry and by the secret culture of the Mysteries gradually transformed into a trued and perfect pyramidal capstone. The temple is complete only when the initiate himself becomes the living apex through which the divine power is focused into the diverging structure below.

W. Marsham Adams calls the Great Pyramid "the House of the Hidden Places"; such indeed it was, for it represented the inner sanctuary of pre-Egyptian wisdom. By the Egyptians the Great Pyramid was associated with Hermes, the god of wisdom and letters and the Divine Illuminator worshiped through the planet Mercury. Relating Hermes to the Pyramid emphasizes anew the fact that it was in reality the supreme temple of the Invisible and Supreme Deity. The Great Pyramid was not a lighthouse, an observatory, or a tomb, but the first temple of the Mysteries, the first structure erected as a repository for those secret truths which are the certain foundation of all arts and sciences. It was the perfect emblem of the *microcosm* and the *macrocosm* and, according to the secret teachings, the tomb of Osiris, the black god of the Nile. Osiris represents a certain manifestation of solar energy, and therefore his house or tomb is emblematic of the universe within which he is entombed and upon the cross of which he is crucified.

Through the mystic passageways and chambers of the Great Pyramid passed the illumined of antiquity. They entered its portals as *men*; they came forth as *gods*. It was the place of the "second birth," the "womb of the Mysteries," and wisdom dwelt in it as God dwells in the hearts of men. Somewhere in the depths of its recesses there resided an unknown being who was called "The Initiator," or "The Illustrious One," robed in blue and gold and bearing in his hand the sevenfold key of Eternity. This was the lion-faced hierophant, the Holy One, the Master of Masters, who never left the House of Wisdom and whom no man ever saw save he who had passed through the gates of preparation and purification. It was in these chambers that Plato--he of the broad brow---came face to face with the wisdom of the ages personified in the Master of the Hidden House.

Who was the Master dwelling in the mighty Pyramid, the many rooms of which signified the worlds in space; the Master whom none might behold save those who had been "born again"? He alone fully knew the secret of the Pyramid, but he has departed the way of the wise and the house is empty. The hymns of praise no longer echo in muffled tones through the chambers; the neophyte no longer passes through the elements and wanders among the seven stars; the candidate no longer receives the "Word of Life" from the lips of the Eternal One. Nothing now remains that the eye of man can see but an empty shell--the outer symbol of an inner truth--and men call the House of God a tomb!

The technique of the Mysteries was unfolded by the Sage Illuminator, the Master of the Secret House. The power to know his guardian spirit was revealed to the new initiate; the method of disentangling his material body from. his divine vehicle was explained; and to consummate the *magnum opus*, there was revealed the Divine Name--the secret and unutterable designation of the Supreme Deity, by the very knowledge of which man and his God are made consciously one. With the giving of the Name, the new initiate became himself a *pyramid*, within the chambers of whose soul numberless other human beings might also receive spiritual enlightenment.

In the King's Chamber was enacted the drama of the "second death." Here the candidate, after being crucified upon the cross of the solstices and the equinoxes, was buried in the great coffer. There is a profound mystery to the atmosphere and temperature of the King's Chamber: it is of a peculiar deathlike cold which cuts to the marrow of the bone. This room was a doorway between the material world and the transcendental spheres of Nature. While his body lay in the coffer, the soul of the neophyte soared as a human-headed hawk through the celestial realms, there to discover first hand the eternity of Life, Light, and Truth, as well as the illusion of Death, Darkness, and Sin. Thus in one sense the Great Pyramid may be likened to a gate through which the ancient priests permitted a few to pass toward the attainment of individual completion. It is also to be noted incidentally that if the coffer in the King's Chamber be struck, the sound emitted has no counterpart in any known musical scale. This tonal value may have formed part of that combination of circumstances which rendered the King's Chamber an ideal setting for the conferment of the highest degree of the Mysteries.

The modern world knows little of these ancient rites. The scientist and the theologian alike gaze upon the sacred structure, wondering what fundamental urge inspired the herculean labor. If they would but think for a moment, they would realize that there is only one urge in the soul of man capable of supplying the required incentive--namely, the desire to know, to understand, and to exchange the narrowness of human mortality for the greater breadth and scope of divine enlightenment. So men say of the Great Pyramid that it is the most perfect building in the world, the source of weights and measures, the original Noah's Ark, the origin of languages, alphabets,. and scales of temperature and humidity. Few realize, however, that it is the gateway to the Eternal.

Though the modern world may know a million secrets, the ancient world knew one--and that one was greater than the million; for the *million* secrets breed death, disaster, sorrow, selfishness, lust, and avarice, but the *one* secret confers life, light, and truth. The time will come when the secret wisdom shall again be the dominating religious and philosophical urge of the world. The day is at hand when the doom of dogma shall be sounded. The great theological Tower of Babel, with its confusion of tongues, was built of bricks of mud and the mortar of slime. Out of the cold ashes of lifeless creeds, however, shall rise *phoenix-like* the ancient Mysteries. No other institution has so completely satisfied the religious aspirations of humanity, for since the destruction of the Mysteries there never has been a religious code to which Plato could have subscribed. The unfolding of man's spiritual nature is as much an exact science as astronomy, medicine or jurisprudence. To accomplish this end religions were primarily established; and out of religion have come science, philosophy, and logic as methods whereby this divine purpose might be realized.

The Dying God shall rise again! The secret room in the House of the Hidden Places shall be rediscovered. The Pyramid again shall stand as the ideal emblem of solidarity, inspiration, aspiration, resurrection, and regeneration. As the passing sands of time bury civilization upon civilization beneath their weight, the Pyramid shall remain as the Visible covenant between Eternal Wisdom and the world. The time may yet come when the chants of the illumined shall be heard once more in its ancient passageways and the Master of the Hidden House shall await in the Silent Place for the coming of that man who, casting aside the fallacies of dogma and tenet, seeks simply Truth and will be satisfied with neither substitute nor counterfeit.

Masonic Hieroglyphics

By George Smith

Egypt, from whence we derive many of our mysteries, has always held a distinguished rank in history, and was once celebrated above all others for its antiquities, learning, opulence, and fertility. Such, however, is the mutability of all sublunary things, that its present has no resemblance of its former state; and those who read the ancient and modern accounts of Egypt, can scarce believe that they appertain to the same country. Its learning and masonic mysteries is changed into ignorance, its opulence to poverty, and its fertility to frequent scarcity. Nevertheless, Egypt affords ample matter for admiration and pity; the explorer of nature and the royal art, as well as the admirer of antiquities, may both gratify the most boundless curiosity, in contemplating the wonderful productions of nature, and the stupendous remains of antiquity.

The noble and sublime secrets of which we are possessed, are contained in our traditions, represented by hieroglyphic figures, and intimated by our symbolical customs and ceremonies; whereby several useful lessons are inculcated for the more ample extension of knowledge, and promotion of virtue and masonry.

The general depravity, and incapacity of mankind, have made it expedient to tyle, and securely conceal our mysteries, or sublime truths, by hieroglyphic and symbolical representations; to prevent their becoming familiar, common and contemptible. For this reason the Egyptians, in the remotest antiquity, adapted, both in their writings and inscriptions, the use of hieroglyphics or mystical characters and symbols, consisting of various animals, the parts of human bodies, and mechanical instruments, by means of which they wrapped up, and concealed their doctrines from the vulgar and unlearned. Hence also, and for the same reason, the wisest nations have ever employed symbolical figures, or occult, allusive representations, to conceal their mysteries. In our tyling, or casting a veil over our mysteries, we imitate the wisdom of the most enlightened periods, and nations. To distinguish a true brother from an impostor, certain tests have been wisely and judiciously invented. These are matters, however, which can by no means be specified, or particularly mentioned, but to the qualified and worthy freemason.

The Egyptian priests regulated the proper symbols, and at the same time the most expressive of the divine attributes; and of the effects of divine Providence in every part of the universe, they studied with great application and care, not only the peculiar properties of those animals, birds and fishes, herbs and plants, which Egypt produced, but also the geometrical properties of lines and figures; by a regular connection of them in various orders, attitudes, and compositions, they formed the whole system of their theology and philosophy, which was hidden under hieroglyphic figures and characters, known only to themselves and to those who were initiated into their mysteries.

In this system their principal hero-gods, Osiris and Isis, theologically represented the supreme Being, and universal nature; and physically signified the two great celestial luminaries, the sun and moon, by whose influence all nature was actuated. In like manner the inferior heroes represented the subordinate gods, who were the ministers of the supreme spirit; and physically they denoted the mundane elements and powers. Their symbols represented, and comprehended under them, the natural productions of the Deity, and the various beneficial effects of divine Providence in the works of creation; and also the order and harmony, the powers and mutual influence of the several parts of the universal system.

This is the sum and substance of the Egyptian learning, so nearly connected with freemasonry, so famed in ancient times throughout the world. And in this general system the particular history of their hero-gods, together with the mystical knowledge of our society, was, and is contained, and applied to physical causes and theological science. The hieroglyphic system was composed with great art and sagacity; and was so universally esteemed and admired, that the most learned philosophers of other nations came into Egypt on purpose to be instructed in it, and to learn the philosophy and theology conveyed by these apposite symbols.

In this hieroglyphic system the hero-gods not only represented, and were symbols of the supreme gods and subordinate deities, but they had each their animal symbol to represent their peculiar power, energy, and administration; and their figures were compounded of one part or other of their symbols to express more sensibly the natural effects of divine energy attributed to them.

Thus Osiris, when he represented the power and all-seeing

providence of the supreme Being, had a human body with a hawk's head, and a scepter in his hand, and decorated with the other regalia, or ensigns of royalty. Under the same form he also represented the sun, the great celestial luminary; and, as it were, the soul of the world; his symbol now was a bull, and the scarabaeus, or beetle, which expressed the sun's motion, by rolling balls of dung, containing its seed, backwards, or from east to west, his face being towards the east. The symbolic bull was likewise of a particular form and make, to denote the various influences of the sun.

Isis was formed with many breasts, to represent the earth, the universal mother, and with a cornucopia in her hand, denoting the nutritive and productive powers of nature; her symbol was a cow, part black and part white, to represent the enlightened and dark parts of the moon.

Hermes had a dog's head, which was his symbol, to denote his sagacity in the invention of arts and sciences; especially in his watchful diligence-in the culture of religious rites and sacred knowledge; at the same time he symbolically represented the divine Providence, was worshipped as the chief counsellor of Saturn and Osiris; he who communicated the will of the gods to men, and by whom their souls were conducted into the other world. He was likewise represented by the Ibis, and with the head of this bird, which was, at the same time, his symbol, to convey his energetic literature to the Egyptians, which they believed was done under the form of this bird, and confined to their nation only, as the Ibis was not known to live any where but in Egypt.

The universal soul itself was beautifully represented by a

winged globe, with a serpent emerging from it. The globe denoted the infinite, divine essence, whose center, to use the expression in the Hermetic writings, was every where, and circumference no where; the wings of the hawk representing the divine, all-comprehensive intellect; and the serpent denoted the vivifying power of God, by which life and existence are given to all things.

Orus was a principal deity of the Egyptians, and, according to his hieroglyphic forms and habits, signified sometimes the sun, and sometimes the harmony of the whole mundane system; at the same time, being the offspring of Osiris and Isis, he was always represented young. In his hieroglyphic figure he was represented with the staff, on the top of which the head of the Upupa, to signify, by the variegated feather of that bird, the beautiful variety of the creation. In one of his hands he held a lituus, to denote the harmony of the system; and a gnomon in the other, to shew the perfect proportion of its parts. Behind him was a triangle inscribed in a circle, to signify that the world was made by the unerring wisdom of God. He had sometimes a cornucopia in his hand, to denote the fertility and production of the earth.

Harpocrates was described holding one of his fingers on his lips, to denote the mysterious and infallible nature of God, and that the knowledge of him was to be sought after with profound and silent meditation.

Upon the whole, almost all the Egyptian deities and symbols centered in two, namely, Osiris and Isis, who represented, .under various hieroglyphic forms, both the celestial and terrestrial system, together with all the divine attributes, operations, and energy, which created, animated, and preserved them.

The Egyptians likewise concealed their moral philosophy under hieroglyphic symbols; but these were not the subjects of the hieroglyphics delineated on the obelisks. And as hieroglyphic and symbolical figures were very ancient in Egypt, and first invented, at least formed into a system there, so they were thence carried into other countries, and initiated in all religious and masonic mysteries, as well as in political and moral science.

Thus the preceding symbolical figures, making the substance of hieroglyphics, and belonging to Osiris, his family and cotemporaries, they were probably formed into a system soon after the death of the hero-gods, by some who had been instructed in the art of hieroglyphics, by Hermes, the inventor of them. The first he formed himself, and the others were probably added by his learned successors, who had been instructed by him in all his mysterious learning.

This hieroglyphic system was in its beginning more simple, and less compounded, than afterwards; for it had been improved for several ages before it appeared on the obelisks of the temples. And hence we may infer the time of the first Egyptian hieroglyphic symbols; for, in all probability, they were not older than the time of the famous Hermes, who flourished in the reign, and some time after the death of Osiris.

The hieroglyphic symbols were in early times carried into Greece, and gave the first occasion to the fables of the poets with regard to the metamorphoses of the gods, which they improved from inventions of their own; and from the knowledge of them the Greeks ascribed peculiar arts and inventions to their gods, whose names they first received from Egypt.

The Egyptians being thus more worthy of masonic attention than any other nation of antiquity, their history being more interesting to us than any other; hence it is from them, by an uninterrupted chain, all the most polite and best constituted nations of Europe have received their first principles of their laws, arts, and sciences. The Egyptians instructed and enlightened the Greeks, who performed the same beneficent-office to the Romans; and these lords of the world were not ashamed to borrow from the Greeks the knowledge which they wanted, which they afterwards communicated to the rest of mankind, and of which we are in possession to this day.

The Egyptians in the earliest ages constituted a great number of lodges, but, with assiduous care, kept their secrets of masonry from all strangers. They wrapped up their mysteries in disguised allusions, enigmas, fables, and allegories; from whence arose our various obscure questions and answers, and many other mystic obscurities, which lead to the royal craft; the true sense of which is practiced by thousands, though understood but by few. These secrets have been imperfectly handed down to us by oral tradition only, and ought to be kept undiscovered to the laborers, craftsmen and apprentices, till, by good behavior and long study, they become better acquainted in geometry and the liberal arts, and thereby qualified for masters and wardens; which is seldom or ever the case with English masons.

The Ancient Mysteries

By Albert G. Mackey

I now propose, for the purpose of illustrating these views, and of familiarizing the reader with the coincidences between Freemasonry and the ancient Mysteries, so that he may be better enabled to appreciate the mutual influences of each on the other as they are hereafter to be developed, to present a more detailed relation of one or more of these ancient systems of initiation.

As the first illustration, let us select the Mysteries of Osiris, as they were practiced in Egypt, the birthplace of all that is wonderful in the arts or sciences, or mysterious in the religion, of the ancient world.

It was on the Lake of Sais that the solemn ceremonies of the Osirian initiation were performed. "On this lake," says Herodotus, "it is that the Egyptians represent by night his sufferings whose name I refrain from mentioning; and this representation they call their Mysteries."

Osiris, the husband of Isis, was an ancient king of the Egyptians. Having been slain by Typhon, his body was cut into pieces by his murderer, and the mangled remains cast upon the waters of the Nile, to be dispersed to the four winds of heaven. His wife, Isis, mourning for the death and the mutilation of her husband, for many days searched diligently with her companions for the portions of the body, and having at length found them, united them together, and bestowed upon them decent interment,--while Osiris, thus restored, became the chief deity of his subjects, and his worship was united with that of Isis, as the fecundating and fertilizing powers of nature. The candidate in these initiations was made to pass through a mimic repetition of the conflict and destruction of Osiris, and his eventual recovery; and the explanations made to him, after he had received the full share of light to which the painful and solemn ceremonies through which he had passed had entitled him, constituted the secret doctrine of which I have already spoken, as the object of all the Mysteries. Osiris,--a real and personal god to the people,--to be worshipped with fear and with trembling, and to be propitiated with sacrifices and burnt offerings, became to the initiate but a symbol of the

"Great first cause, least understood,"

while his death, and the wailing of Isis, with the recovery of the body, his translation to the rank of a celestial being, and the consequent rejoicing of his spouse, were but a tropical mode of teaching that after death comes life eternal, and that though the body be destroyed, the soul shall still live.

"Can we doubt," says the Baron Sainte Croix, "that such ceremonies as those practiced in the Mysteries of Osiris had been originally instituted to impress more profoundly on the mind the dogma of future rewards and punishments?"

"The sufferings and death of Osiris," says Mr. Wilkinson, "were the great Mystery of the Egyptian religion; and some traces of it are perceptible among other people of antiquity. His being the divine goodness and the abstract idea of 'good,' his manifestation upon earth (like an Indian god), his death and resurrection, and his office as judge of the dead in a future state, look like the early revelation of a future manifestation of the deity converted into a mythological fable."

A similar legend and similar ceremonies, varied only as to time, and place, and unimportant details, were to be found in all the initiations of the ancient Mysteries. The dogma was the same,--future life,--and the method of inculcating it was the same. The coincidences between the design of these rites and that of Freemasonry, which must already begin to appear, will enable us to give its full value to the expression of Hutchinson, when he says that "the Master Mason represents a man under the Christian doctrine saved from the grave of iniquity and raised to the faith of salvation."

In Phoenicia similar Mysteries were celebrated in honor of Adonis, the favorite lover of Venus, who, having, while hunting, been slain by a wild boar on Mount Lebanon, was restored to life by Proserpine. The mythological story is familiar to every classical scholar. In the popular theology, Adonis was the son of Cinyras, king of Cyrus, whose untimely death was wept by Venus and her attendant nymphs: in the physical theology of the philosophers, he was a symbol of the sun, alternately present to and absent from the earth; but in the initiation into the Mysteries of his worship, his resurrection and return from Hades were adopted as a type of the immortality of the soul. The ceremonies of initiation in the Adonia began with lamentation for his loss,--or, as the prophet Ezekiel expresses it, "Behold, there sat women weeping for Thammuz,"--for such was the name under which his worship was introduced among the Jews; and they ended with the most extravagant demonstrations of joy at the representation of his return to life, while the hierophant exclaimed, in a congratulatory strain,--

"Trust, ye initiates; the god is safe,
And from our grief salvation shall arise."

Before proceeding to an examination of those Mysteries which are the most closely connected with the masonic institution, it will be as well to take a brief view of their general organization.

The secret worship, or Mysteries, of the ancients were always divided into the lesser and the greater; the former being intended only to awaken curiosity, to test the capacity and disposition of the candidate, and by symbolical purifications to prepare him for his introduction into the greater Mysteries.

The candidate was at first called an aspirant, or seeker of the truth, and the initial ceremony which he underwent was a lustration or purification by water. In this condition he may be compared to the Entered Apprentice of the masonic rites, and it is here worth adverting to the fact (which will be hereafter more fully developed) that all the ceremonies in the first degree of masonry are symbolic of an internal purification.

In the lesser Mysteries the candidate took an oath of secrecy, which was administered to him by the mystagogue, and then received a preparatory instruction, which enabled him afterwards to understand the developments of the higher and subsequent division. He was now called a *Mystes*, or initiate, and may be compared to the Fellow Craft of Freemasonry.

In the greater Mysteries the whole knowledge of the divine truths, which was the object of initiation, was communicated. Here we find, among the various ceremonies which assimilated these rites to Freemasonry, the *aphanism*, which was the disappearance or death; the *pastos*, the couch, coffin, or grave; the *euresis*, or the discovery of the body; and the *autopsy*, or full sight of everything, that is, the complete communication of the secrets. The candidate was here called an *epopt*, or eye-witness, because nothing was now hidden from him; and hence he may be compared to the Master Mason, of whom Hutchinson says that "he has discovered the knowledge of God and his salvation, and been redeemed from the death of sin and the sepulchre of pollution and unrighteousness."

www.ingramcontent.com/pod-product-compliance
Lightning Source LLC
LaVergne TN
LVHW041459070426
835507LV00009B/703